I Love You-Mom *Forever!!!!*

A Mother's Love is a gorgeous blanket that is wrapped in love and carries you through life.

Ann Marie Kim

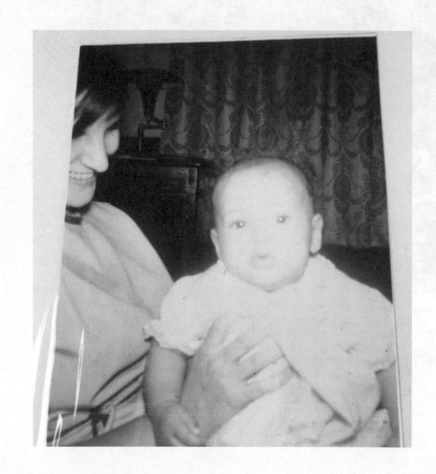

Balboa Press books may be ordered through booksellers or by contacting:

Balboa Press
A Division of Hay House
1663 Liberty Drive
Bloomington, IN 47403
www.balboapress.com
844-682-1282

ISBN: 979-8-7652-4673-3 (sc)
ISBN: 979-8-7652-4674-0 (hc)
ISBN: 979-8-7652-4672-6 (e)

Library of Congress Control Number: 2023920846

Print information available on the last page.

Balboa Press rev. date: 01/23/2024

BALBOA.PRESS
A DIVISION OF HAY HOUSE

Introduction

This book is dedicated to the precious memory of my Mother, Barbara Ann Caruso- Smith born on January 22, 1941, in the West - End (Little Italy), of Boston, Massachusetts and passed away the morning of October 22, 2018, in Brighton, Massachusetts. My Mother was one of the most loving, kind, generous and gorgeous women I have ever known. Her memory of love, kindness, tenacity and a fierce love for her children and husband shall forever be etched within my heart and soul forever. My Mother had the capacity to decipher the complete character of an individual within seconds of meeting them. Mom, I miss you completely, your love, your straightforwardness, you never 'beat around the bush', you were truthful, honest, direct and filled with integrity, which for me is very refreshing, as I always 'knew where I stood' with you. The world needs more precious souls like you, Mom, filled with honesty, truth and love.

I wish we had more time together. The Bible speaks of how quickly our lives pass by and I never truly allowed those words to sink into my soul, until I witnessed first hand, you passing away. In retrospect, Mom, your life flew by.

Mom, as I texted Marcia, your wonderful grafted in daughter, I expressed these words to her. 'Truly, this book writes itself from the tablets of love stored upon my heart over the years… basking in the beauty of her great presence.'

Your precious nephew gently reminded me that God does not give us more than what we can handle. I agreed with him and said, "I am fine, my heart is just overflowing with love, gratitude and utter appreciation for having spent a lifetime with one of the most incredible human beings on the planet. THE MOST INCREDIBLE MOM EVER!!!!!!

Mom here is a picture of the Island of Capri, right next door to Naples Italy.
Simpy Gorgeous!

God, what do I say, where shall I begin? Tears run down my cheeks as I stare at this beautiful, beautiful picture on the cover of this book. Look at the inexpressible joy on my mother's face and the most beautiful smile and gorgeous brown eyes I have ever witnessed, even to this day. This precious smile greeted me during my first minutes, seconds on earth, those loving hands and heart took care of me and made me into the incredible woman I am today. Thank you Mom. I know I have expressed these words with you in person, however, I decided to write them down forever, so that the next generation and those of us who you have left behind (in your beautiful wake of love) may still have the honor of your memory and love etched within our hearts and souls forever.

Tethered

Mom, I am convinced our hearts were tethered to each other even before we came into existence, even before my arrival in your womb. I remember you telling me stories of when I was a baby, with one strand of red hair on my head…how I would cry when you closed the door for me to go to sleep. However, as soon as I saw your face, I would start to smile. I am confident, even at that age your presence gave my soul an incredible sense of peace and assurance that I was not alone. Mom, thank you for believing in me and loving me unconditionally. All of your love, strength and belief in my abilities has given me 'wings to soar' like the wings of a beautiful bald eagle, I so adore.

Thank you Mom for telling me the truth, when during certain times of my life, especially as a teenager and young adult, I did not care to hear it. Thank you for sharing your love and kindness with me, even though you had three more children and a husband to share this with. In some amazing way, one in which I have yet to understand, God gave you enough love for all of us.

Mom, I know you are in heaven now sharing eternity with the Ancient of Days and for this I am eternally grateful. I love the way God has created Mom's, especially you, Mom. He created you with so much love that it literally covers my soul like a blanket. This special blanket of love has and continues to enable me to walk through this journey of life, basically unscathed by the busyness, concerns and worries of the world.

Little One

I remember back to the age of six (6), when I would ride the local bus with you. Ironically, I would sit up front, yes, this little mulatto girl, who had no idea at this age what our country was facing with the Civil Rights Movement and all. Growing up, I never understood racism, as I witnessed first hand how you and Dad loved each other. You taught me how to respect others and race was never a qualifier of who to be respectful to. Thank you, Mom for teaching me how to pay attention to landmarks to find my way back home on the bus…which years later would prove extremely valuable, as it enabled me to navigate my way around the city of Boston and literally the world.

Today, I travel to a special place once a year, as your eldest sister Aunt Rose encouraged me to do years ago. Mom, please give Aunt Rose and Grandma, Grandpa and all of our relatives and love ones a hug and kiss for me. I know you must be happy to finally be able to spend much missed time with your Mom in heaven. Thank you for naming me after her! (Anna Maria)

Teenage

Mom, I remember you enrolling me in the Barbizon School of Modeling because you wanted me to have more confidence and not continue to be a tomboy competing with Dad and my brothers in sports. Thank you for the healthy balance and for expressing to me over and over again how gorgeous I am and to ignore the unkind commentary of those girls in school or in our neighborhood who shared opposite points of view.

Thank you, Mom for being there at every important event in my life back then. For my 8th grade, high school and college graduation. I wish I could bottle up your smile and take it with me forever. Your smile and love are so infectious Mom.

Adult

As I applied for jobs after college and landed a job in downtown Boston, I broke your heart by joining a church, which I now realize was not truly based on biblical standards of honoring one's Mother and Father. Later, I spent many years making up the lost time with you. Thank you Mom, for loving me through each stage of life. Honestly, Mothers are not rewarded enough for all that they endure with their children, even as their children become adults and make decisions on occasion that may not resonate with the way, you Mom, would have preferred things…. your unconditional love mended any misunderstanding.

You bring each one of us back as though only a day has passed, laughing, making forya (an Italian dish of scrambled eggs with parmesan cheese); no one makes it quite like you, Mom. Or green peppers with eggs…yum. I miss you Mom, your smile, the sound of your voice, laughing, the smell of your hair, awakening to the lovely aroma of your Italian sauce on Sunday mornings.

Truly Grateful

Mom, I am truly grateful to God for the life you created for us all. Our life centered around endless lively conversations and incredibly delicious food that both you and Dad made for us. You, Mom, in my opinion and mind you, by now I have traveled to Italy several times and have had food in the North-end of Boston (Little Italy).

Mom, your Italian dishes are equal to, or more excellent than the ones in Milan, Italy and Boston's North-end. I love the way you, regardless of if someone else was in the middle of sharing a story… would start sharing a story of your own, totally oblivious (or at least so you pretended) to interrupting someone else's story. The house was always filled with such laughter and love. Honestly, I do not know how Dad survives in that home alone. After you passed away, I have been over several times and I sit in your seat, perhaps, in a way to feel closer to you…in an attempt to ease the pain of losing you. As I sit there and listen to the conversations, it is not the same.

The Transition

As I sit here in my home in the country, peering out over the prairie watching the sunrise…I realized, although the time seemed a lot longer, you literally passed away within three months.

I had just arrived back from England to visit a long time friend. Two days prior to my arrival I received a text message from my baby sister who said, Mom is not acting normal. I think we may need to rush her to the hospital. Apparently, you had been up all night stating that this entity was attempting to kill you. None of us (family members) with the exception of Dad realized how truly sick you were.

Each day, you would share how these entities were following you. I thought for certain that it may have been associated with the large cataract the doctors removed back in February, 2018, when I flew to Boston to take you in for surgery. We discovered after finishing the prescription of the eye drops, you still saw these entities. As I write this particular piece, the sun is peeking out over the horizon and I must admit, this is one of the most beautiful sunrises I have witnessed in a while. The rays of light are elegantly illuminating the sky, Mom, I am sure you have something to do with this. I love you Mom, Forever!

How do I say thank you to the first precious soul who held me in the hospital upon my birth and shared that incredibly beautiful smile with me. The smile that lights up my life forever. Oh, how my heart misses you, Mom. No one in this world can ever replace you.

How does one thank their Mom, for teaching them how to take their first step, for providing a home filled with love, protection, a shelter, a safe haven. How does one even begin to express their unending gratitude to be blessed so incredibly with such a Mother. How, Mom?

I wish as a child, I was more aware of the entire process of life. I would have encouraged you back then. I would have become your biggest fan, as you were mine. Mom, I do not think that we realize how fast life flies by. I apologize if at any Moment I took you for granted, or if you felt I took you for granted.

Cookie Crumb

I remember one time, I asked (since you always call me 'My Cookie Crumb') why I had to be the crumbs, instead of the cookie. You leaned over on your chair and explained, as though you were telling me one of the best kept secrets in the world, how the cookie crumbs are the best part of the cookie, because you want to enjoy every last crumb.

My soul beamed once I heard your explanation of, "My Cookie Crumb." Several years prior to your passing, you starting ending our conversations with, 'I love you More'. I believe Michael Jackson used to say this? Mom, what a precious way to end a conversation, I love you More as well…forever, for all eternity.

Mom, I miss your voice. I wish I had recorded it more, especially the birthday and Valentine's Day wishes you left on my voicemail each year.

I miss hearing your stories about how you waited on number 70 or whichever number for $100, $300 or the coverall. I miss hearing your stories about playing cards with Eunice (one of your life long best friends).

Mom, I am not sure if you remember any of this…however, Leeanne visited you several times at the hospital. Mom, the love you expressed when you saw Leeanne was so beautiful. You tilted your head and held her with your precious arms. Leeanne gently placed your new warm sweater on you and rolled up your sleeves. Mom this was a truly priceless Moment, embedded in love.

Soul Talking

Mom, I believe you had this quality as well….I remember hearing stories of how your Higher Self told you something would happen, for example, the knowing of your Mom passing within two weeks. Well, I believe the trait may be hereditary (smile). For some reason, back in February, when I flew home to take you in for the cataract surgery, God told me that you would not be alive on or before October 25, 2018. I ignored the thought and instead, started praying and fasting, begging God to extend your life for fifteen (15) years as He did with King Hezekiah.

I started to incorporate steps as I do within my profession, steps on how do we fix you, Mom. I contacted one of my precious best friends who is a doctor and shared your symptoms with her. Immediately, she diagnosed the symptoms as Lewy Body Dementia.

At this point, I had never heard of the medical term Lewy Body Dementia. I started reading everything I could and ironically, on the flight back home to Boston on October 19th, I watched a movie about Robin Williams, who apparently passed away from the same disease.

You, Mom, filled all of our hearts with love, laughter and a great conversation and I would give anything to hear those stories again today!

Upon Annette rushing you to the Emergency Room at Beth Israel, the head psychiatrist pre-diagnosed you with the same thing. All of us wanted you to receive the best treatment possible and our overall goal as a family was to have you stable on dementia meds and walking again, so that you would be able to live at home with Dad and have a visiting nurse and home health care aide taking care of you.

We did not realize that you had been exhibiting these behaviors for several years. Dad never shared this with us. He said he did not want to place you in a nursing home. He would rather take care of you himself. God bless him for his efforts. He had no idea what the Lewy Body Dementia did to your mind and only time would show him.

We miraculously convinced your doctor to allow you to go home, since you always took your meds for Dad and always ate your meals without any issues. As I sat beside you and Dad sat across from you in the community room at the hospital, it was priceless to witness you speaking with the social worker on how much Dad takes great care of you and how he is such an excellent cook. Very important to us, right Mom, especially, with your Italian heritage.

Struggling with not Being there at the Final Hour.

Mom, I have played this particular scene over and over again in my mind, thinking, wow, I really wanted to be there with you to hold your hand and kiss your face during the final hours. I kept beating myself up inside for not spending the night and leaving with Leeanne instead. Well, yesterday, January 7, 2019, as I was leaving the library, one of the library personnel, of whom I have and continue to visit with for the twelve years I have lived in this area, said she has read in several books that when someone is passing away, they wait until all of their loved ones have left the room and then they pass. I feel now, a true sense of relief. I believe you knew that I would walk through fire for you Mommy.

Message of Love

My message to everyone is to love your children, young adults, and full grown adults completely. Decide to listen to them, to be there for them…as you show them this example, your children will know how to truly love you.

Mom, thank you for being such an example to me and my siblings. Thank you for showing us how to truly love. Thank you for holding my hand as a child, being patient with me with all of my concerns, which may have been minor, however enormous in my eyes at the time. This time though, I am holding your hand, I am looking into your eyes and telling you how valuable you are, how much I love you and how you are literally, the Best Mom anyone may truly have.

A Memorial in your Honor

For your Memorial I had to set everything up by myself. Mike, the kind gentleman knocked on the door at 9:30 am, the morning of your Memorial. He wanted to know how the chairs and tables would be set up. I had left these details to Annette, however, she had an impacted wisdom tooth that was removed the day before. So, I called her on FaceTime and we both worked with Mike to set up the chairs and tables.

Dad did not help one bit with the set up. I believe he was hurting so badly that he could not bring himself to the finality of it all. Mom, I am sure you see him from heaven, sitting there on the couch playing all of those romantic songs, as he thinks of you. Later in the evening of your Memorial, Leeanne, Jianna, Ann and I came over and he was sitting there listening to love songs with tears running down his precious face.

Earlier in the day, since God knew I needed help to set up the Community room for your Memorial…God sent your favorite niece in all of the world, Lacye Marie and her wonderful husband David to help me. Then, your favorite nephews Larry and John showed up shortly later along with Larry's wife Tracy and John's girlfriend who helped out tremendously. Auntie Katie, of course was there, a complete image of you. Wow! The DNA strand in your family tree runs strong.

How fortunate were you Mom, to be with the love of your life for sixty (60) years. Even then, you did not believe the time was long enough. As each time Dad visited you at the various hospitals and nursing homes over the three months, you placed your hand in his and said, 'Come on, let's go. ' Even the day before your passing, you placed your hand in his for the very last time and said, 'Come on, let's go.'

Mom, my heart goes out to both you and Dad! Your legacy of love for each other, even though it may have ended on the physical plane, lives on for eternity on the spiritual plane. Mom, I miss you so much. I wish you were here for me to give you endless kisses on your face. Oh, Mom, I cry endlessly because I just wanted to save you. I wanted to make everything fine again. If I had the power to heal you and bring you back to perfect health and happiness, I would do just that, within a heart beat.

Hearts in the snow

Days Gone By

Mom, I literally cannot believe you are no longer here. I miss you more than words may express. In the early morning hours, as I went to the rest room, I saw a heart shaped on my garage roof and I immediately knew that was you telling me how much you love me.

You see, earlier that evening, I was watching a Christmas special and one of the songs that was sung reminded me of us…growing up and many Christmas' past. This Christmas shall never be the same without you.

I miss your laugh, your smile, hearing about your day, giving you endless kisses on your cheeks only to witness how much you love receiving all of the love, affection and attention. Mom, I just wanted to save you. I wanted to remove all of the pain and restore you back to complete and perfect health.

Sometimes, my mind plays back every scene over the last year and a half. I wanted to let you know by my being there that I was taking care of you. Even when your precious mind would wander into that awful Lewy Body Dementia world, I listened intently to every word you spoke, and even paid very close attention to your facial expressions during the times you could not speak.

I shared with Annette the other day how you went ahead of us into heaven, so that when we arrive you'll show us around and we shall not be lost. Changing my thoughts and thinking this way helps me make it through these long days without you.

I notice heart shaped clouds when I fly and a gentle tap on my shoulder once, I believe this is your spirit telling me how much you love me. I prayed the other day for God to take very good care of you in heaven and to please be sure to take your hand in His to show you the way to the new heaven He intends to create, when Jesus Christ, whose name is Yeshua in Hebrew, comes back.

Whenever I have an opportunity, I encourage people everywhere to cherish their loved ones. Mom, I believe you went to be with God a little too early. I know that we are all knit together in our Mother's womb and each day written for us has already been completed by God. You left too soon!

Sometimes, life unfolds in a manner we may not understand. As for now, Mom, I have dedicated the next year to dancing for you…since you could not walk for the last three months of your physical life here on earth. I pray Mom that this is where God wants me for now. I am also praying and thanking God in advance for sending the perfect people along my path for my Inspirational Speaking career to take off and for my words to encourage souls all over the planet. I am not completely sure how heaven works, however, if you can see me typing this…Mom, I love you more than several universes stringed together, and more than a billion sunsets and sunrises.

Mom Thank you for

1. Believing in me since the day I showed up on the planet.
2. For being my biggest cheer leader and biggest fan…always telling me how proud you were of me.
3. For believing that I could become anything I placed my mind to.
4. For believing that I am gorgeous not just because I am your daughter.
5. For sharing on countless occasions how I am perfect exactly as I am.
6. For your great smile, hugs and kisses.
7. For your love that covers my soul and my siblings as a blanket, keeping our hearts warm, safe and secure.
8. Your love enables us to go through life fully equipped to partake in this beautiful journey.
9. Your smile turns any gloomy day into one of the most beautiful days ever.
10. Your love of people and fine cuisine turns any gathering into one lovely festival.
11. Your love of your culture, of where you have been and where you were headed is the essence and beauty of who you are to me.

Mom, you may not have known this, I shared and continue to share about what my nationality is. Especially, since I know how important it was to you. I am so proud to be 50% Italian, I am so proud, honored and humbled to have you as my Mother. I check off the 'other 'box' and explain via percentages what portion of my ethnicity is. I understand now, the laws of our country attempted not to embrace who someone truly is, if they happened to be a mixture of beautiful races.

Thanks to you, I have and am continuing to learn how to love myself. I think this is a very important quality to possess as a young girl, teenager, lady and woman. The importance of having incredible role models in ones life and the immense love of ones Mother allows her children to 'scale a wall','as King David did in the Bible.

Thank you Mom for living life to the fullest. To be completely present in the Moment. To dominating any conversation with your rendition of a story. For your infectious laugh and how much you love to win at playing cards for pennies or just for fun with Dad and your Bingo friends. Thank you for showing all of us how to truly love. You loved Dad during one of the most severe political and Civil unrests this country has faced and did not yield to the empty dictation of a society gone mad. One where authorities and political figures did not view all lives and races as equal before the mighty throne of God. You chose to love Dad and have a beautiful family of mixed (mulatto) babies regardless of the times. What a pioneer, a truly brave one, I must add.

Mom, what is heaven like? I read in my Bible today in the book of Daniel, how the Ancient of Days, took His seat and how there are thousands upon ten thousand of Angels singing Holy, Holy, Holy to God. I am certain it is truly marvelous to behold. I am going to have to create a plan for my life, for the next five years or so. I wish to make you even prouder of me. (smile) I intend to hold Workshops, Seminars and Conferences on teaching precious souls everywhere how to live the dreams that have been placed within their hearts. I also intend to write a few more wonderful books, I know God has many more words for me to share with the world.

1-11-2019

Mom I just looked at the picture of you holding me on the cover of this book I am dedicating to you. I love your radiant smile. I love the way my little hand holds onto your hand. I love how I had the honor to hold your hand in mine, sort of returning the favor of our life long journey together. Mom, if I could turn back time, even for a 'nano second' and erase all of the times we had disagreements…I would trade those times in for more time with you.

Holding Mom's Hand

As I examine the beautiful details of the picture on this book and how my little hand was holding yours as you held me…my mind rushes back to October 20th when I asked the nurse Megan to take a picture of me holding your hand now, as you rest there in your bed in the ICU. Yes, Mom, the little hand you held so many years ago is now here to hold your hand, speaking comforting words to you…letting you know that everything is going to be okay.

Ironically, as children, we have no idea how life really works. Thank goodness, God created us this way so that we may take time to enjoy each phase of life. It would be rather challenging to know as a child that one day your Mom would not be on the planet.

I believe as adults, we realize this, however, Mom, it does not truly hit home until one experiences it. Now, I completely understand how much you missed your Mother. God sent me an Instagram picture of Jesus holding His hand out with a caption saying, It is time.

Mom, I read it and said, no God, I am not ready for my Mom to leave this planet. The date of this message was October 17, 2018, two days prior to you being admitted into the ICU at St. Elizabeth's hospital.

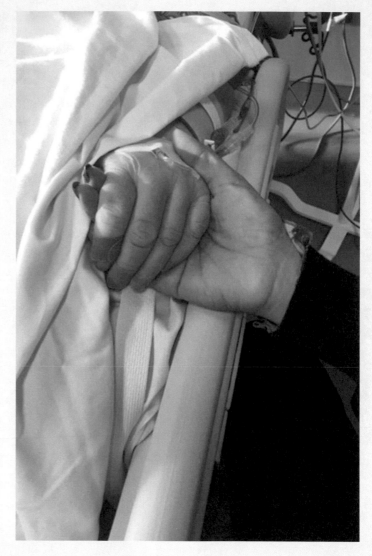

Leaving Us.

Mom, look at Annette's face …she is completely gorgeous, however, this picture speaks a thousand words. She knows, Mom, she knows you are leaving us. Annette has a look of utter disdain on her face. She is 'not having it'. She is not ready for you to leave us. I understand this look completely. We have all tried everything to prolong your life. Anyone of us would 'walk through fire' for you.

Later, when I showed 'Auntie Julie' this picture of Annette, Auntie Julie did a double take as she studied the picture. She exclaimed, 'oh, my! goodness, I honestly thought this was a picture of your Mom at age 16.' I thought to myself, wow, only Auntie Julie, Auntie Katy and Dad would know what you looked like at age 16.

Clock on the Wall

Auntie Katy shared about how the clock on the wall fell. She said the same exact thing happened when your Dad passed away.

I called her to wish her a Happy Thanksgiving and Merry Christmas and New Year. Mommy, she explained how she knew her sister would never want to live that way, being hospitalized and not able to care for herself, walk or be independent as you were your entire life.

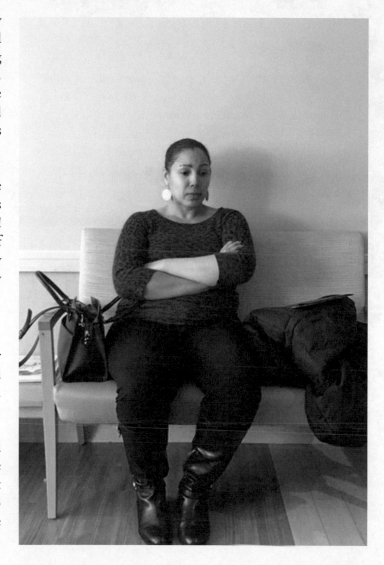

She explained how you loved to go, go, go. This is so true, for someone who never drove a car, you were gone all of the time, shopping at the Mall, Bingo with your girlfriends. I am glad you enjoyed yourself and made so many of us happy by your mere presence. You shall always live in my heart, forever!

Not ready to say Goodbye.

Your Best Friend

Mom, Eunice called me the other day. What a great friend you have in her. She was so sweet. She brought your Bingo bag to Bingo along with one of your dobbers and she won $100. I gave her them when I was sorting through your belongings. (One of the most painful tasks I have ever had to complete). She said she looked up to heaven and said, this one is for you Barbara. Mom, I hope they have Bingo, Papa Gino's pizza with a side of french fries and hot chocolate in heaven for you. Here is a toast to you, one delicious cup of hot chocolate.

Not ready to say Goodbye.

I knew you were passing away the next day as God had placed on my heart when I arrived late that evening on October 19th. On Sunday, as soon as the doctors removed the breathing apparatus and you were able to talk, the first thing you asked for was a french fry. You were gazing at Dad on FaceTime and said, french fry. I knew you were asking for your favorite food prior to heading to heaven. I said in my heart, No God, let her live.

After all of these years, I know based on my experience and walking with the Lord that when He tells you something is going to happen, it shall happen, exactly at His appointed time. I just wanted more time with you. We all wanted more time with you.

I spoke with a friend the other evening and we both agreed that we had the Most Incredible Mom's ever, Moms who loved us with every morsel of their beings. Instead of crying endless oceans, I am now focusing on how fortunate I am, how fortunate Annette, Jimmy and Johnny are for having such a Mom as you. How fortunate Dad is to have been married to such an exemplary woman. You are an incredible human being Mom!

A few months ago, I traveled with my friend Rikki to a little town named Carver. It was quite charming. I decided to have one of our favorite drinks, a hot chocolate. Here's to you Mom!

Mom, it takes everything I have inside of me to move forward with life. Each time something happens, I instinctively want to pick up my phone to call you. I want to tell you all about what has occurred. I guess if I were to give advice to others who still have their Moms and Dads here, I would say, film them. Spend quality time with your folks. Personally, I believe you may never say, I love you too much. I know for you Mom, you loved hearing those words from all of us.

1. Take the trips you always wanted to take with your parents now, when they are still alive and healthy.
2. Choose not to waste time disagreeing about anything. Truly, when it is all said and done the most important factor in life is Love.
3. One may never take back the words they have said to another, so be certain your words are filled with love and laced with kindness.
4. Decide to allow your parents to share their stories, their memories (without interrupting them); smile and bask in the knowing that you are giving them a chance to bask in the beauty of who all of you are collectively as a family, as part of the bond of love.
5. Dance in the rain with your folks. Share all of the good things that are occurring in their lives.
6. Tell each one how precious they are to you. Return the favor of kindness, the favor of combing her hair.
7. Sit beside her bed or chair and listen to her explain your genealogy for the hundredth time.
8. There will be a day when you wished you recorded it so you may play it over and over again.
9. Cherish, Cherish, Cherish them. Both your Mom and Dad did the best they could in raising you and your siblings, let them know how much you appreciate them.
10. Thank each for being there for you.

I am so blessed, honored and fortunate to have such an incredible Mom like yourself. Thank you for giving me your Gorgeous looks and for showing me what it looks like to be brave.

Thank you for showing me unconditional love, kindness and strength. Attributes I shall have with me for all eternity. I love you Mom. To me and in my eyes, you are the best Mom any- one may ever have in this world.

Confidence

Thank you Mom for sending me to modeling school to convince me of how beautiful or as you like to say, how gorgeous I am, a powerful reminder of erasing all of the harsh words the kids in school would say when they discovered my Mom is Italian. Mom, I personally believe mixed or mulatto babies are the best! Whenever, I am traveling or running errands and notice a mixed couple with children or even just a mixed couple I wish them a wonderful life on every level. Actually, I wish everyone this, however, I share with the mixed couple of how I appreciate them, since I am an incredible result of a mixed marriage.

Over the past year and a half, I watched you Mom, what I like to call an incredible human being fight to live in the final chapter of her most precious life.

You were so graceful to total strangers, telling each one how beautiful or kind they were. Honestly, before you became really ill, I marveled at how you were so kind to people who I would have run in the other direction from. Even during your last days on the planet, with your mind ebbing away from the Lewy Body Dementia, you complimented nurses, doctors, aides, anyone who came across your path. Mom, you are my hero, thank you for being a 'walking bill board' on charm, kindness, grace and love .Here is a picture from my modeling years, in Copley Square, across from my favorite library and where Dad lives now.

The Last Two Years

Mom, I wished I realized sooner that you were saying goodbye to us over the last two years. Dad would often say how you kept bringing up your childhood, or talked about your Mom and Dad. I realize how important it was for you to explain all of these things to us.

Mom, there are countless pictures with Dad, where you, Mom, look like a super star, stepping into your glamorous world. No one could even light a candle to your beauty. You were always the "Belle of the Ball." Dad looks like the happiest man in the world sitting beside you.

How much you loved your Mother; How you always were there at home with her just incase she became ill. I realized the other day that you were only twenty-three (23) years old when your Mom passed. Wow, this is such a young age. You were incredibly strong and fierce back then. I am certain the kindnesses of God and His powerful Angels carried you through that time when you lost your Mother. God also gave you children to ease the pain over the years.

Mom, your love is Fierce. I believe you had the strength to go on because we were all born and quite young when your Mom passed. I shall imitate your strength here…. as it is the only way to live life fully now that my cookie crumb is in Heaven walking along the streets of gold and basking in the Beauty of the presence of God.

Geriatric Center

I had the opportunity to tell you that you are the Most Incredible Mom Ever, you stopped and looked up from the sheet you were holding in your hand and said 'Thank you.' To me, it was the most beautiful 'Thank you' I have ever heard in my Life.

Two Days before Saying Goodbye

What I found amazing was when your nephew was visiting you in the ICU. He and his girlfriend decided to go back in after the doctors had to change one of your bandages.

I decided to sit in the waiting room and finish my sandwich I was attempting to eat all day, as no one is permitted to bring food in the ICU. As I sat there eating the sandwich, he runs into the waiting area and says, 'Cuz, your Mom has her eyes open.' I jump up, run into the ICU area placing my sandwich on the counter and ran down the hall to your room 223 (Mom, I woke up the other night exactly at this time in the morning and thought of you, immediately). As I stood by your bed, yes, in fact your eyes were open and you were looking at me.

I said hello Ms. America, as I always do, because you are so truly beautiful to me on every level. Mom, you are one of the kindest, most loving and non-racist human being I know. You treat everyone with lots of respect, regardless of who they are. Your friend Lateria was from Jamaica, your best friend Eunice is from Atlanta (I believe). Auntie Julie is Irish (she is one of your best friends who as children we called Auntie Julie). Mom, had I realized this would be the last weekend I would be able to spend with you, I would have been with you for the entire month prior.

I am truly fortunate to be an entrepreneur, to have the privilege to work for myself and to have taken the end of July and the remaining part of the summer off to be there with you in Boston. Mom, I would not trade that time in for anything in the world.

Back to the ICU hospital room, me looking at you as John Charles explains how he had been calling, (Auntie Barbara, Auntie Barbara, wake up, it is me, John, I am here with my girlfriend to see you). He said he then told you that Ann Marie is here. At that Moment, you opened your eyes and started looking around the room for me.

I could not overcome the urge to cry, so I bent over and gave you a kiss and excused myself. I went into the bathroom next to your bed and started to cry.

Infectious Smile

I pray I have said to you more than all of the grains on the seashore and more than all of the stars inthe evening sky, how much I Love You, Mom!

I hope you realize how much you are treasured and how I love spending every single moment while visiting at home doting over you. You are simply marvelous. I love your infectious smile and the way you interact with people. I have learned how to be kind and lovely even to the most unpleasant human beings solely based on your example. Mom, you can literally charm an entire wasps nest without acquiring one single sting.

Airports

Mom, in the above picture, I just arrived at Logan airport, late Friday night on October 19, 2018, awaiting the arrival of an uber to take me to the ICU to see you. God had already communicated with my spirit that your last day would be on Monday, early morning.

The picture of the gentleman beside me, is a picture of Patrick. Mom, on my travels to one of my IT Consulting Engagements, Patrick was another passenger on the plane who sat down next to me. I always wish people a wonderful life on every level and I had wished Patrick the same. We chatted about work, our clients and then, I shared how you were passing away quickly before my eyes. I shared how frustrating it was to be in a position of not being able to help save you. Mom, I believe God sent Patrick that day and even after you passed to encourage my soul. He shared this precious story about his Grandpa being sick and how his Mom, being a nurse was in the room when the doctor explained to his Grandpa how he only had a few days to live. Once the doctor left the room, his Grandpa looked over at his daughter (Patricks Mom who is a nurse) and said, explain it to me straight. His precious daughter explained all the medical terms the doctor had communicated earlier and how he only had two days to live. Patrick's Grandpa looked his daughter in the eyes and said, well, I guess there is nothing I can do about it.

Mom, for some reason those words, "Well, there is nothing I can do about it," resonated with my soul and gave my heart permission to 'surrender' to the will of God, to the ebb and flow of your precious life and to be at peace with everything. Mom, Patrick was so kind to allow me to take his picture when I saw him in the airport after you passed away and he has given me permission to include it here…to show the world another one of God's angels.

Last Day Before Saying Goodbye:

Mom, you have definitely Written Your Story of love on my heart forever. I shall treasure each page, decade of the love etched into each one of the pages. Thank you for being who you are…thank you for showing me what Love truly looks like. Thank you for loving each of us so much, from Dad, to each one of my siblings (Jimmy, Johnny, Annette) to Fervin, Leeanne, Jianna to Lacye Marie, Larry, John Charles) to Auntie Katy, Auntie Julie, Marcia, Eunice. All of us and so many countless others have been graced by your presence and your incredible love. We all thank you and love you for Eternity.

Mom, gone to Heaven.

Mom, out of privacy for you, during your last days on the planet with us, I have not included any of the pictures of you during your illness. Instead, I have a section of pictures of the sky (right outside your window) over looking Brighton Center, your home for countless years. I also included pictures from your Memorial .

Two Souls who would meet as teenagers marry and spend sixty (60) years together in love, endurance, patience and kindness. Mom, what I think is really hilarious is that the picture of Dad above, he is posing as if he is the 'cat's meow,' when, in fact we know that you were the 'cat's meow,' who captivated his heart.

<u>I know your face anywhere.</u>

A few days ago, I was reading my Bible (I enjoy reading the 365 Day a Year) Bible, the New International Ver-sion. I came upon a scripture when Jesus was addressing the crowd and explained how when our soul goes to be with God, we are neither married or given in marriage, instead, we become like the angels.

My heart was so thrilled to read that passage and I am convinced just as you were crowned Queen of Angels here is this precious picture so many years ago…God has made you Queen of the Angels in Heaven. I love you immensely my Queen

Mom, I am so very grateful for you having taken this picture with Grandma (Ann Marie), I was named after her. The only grandchild from the sixteen (16) children she had, you named me after her. What an honor Mom! I was only two months old here with Grandma and Grandpa. How precious.

Thank you for naming me after your Mother, Anna Maria Caruso. Here she is, this incredible human being who gave birth to you and raised you into the phenomenal woman you were while on this planet. Thank you Grandmother, Anna Maria, the love you poured into my Precious Mom, has most certainly been passed onto several generations. I love you very much as well.

Mommy, I love this picture of you with Grandma and Grandpa. Ann Marie & Charlie Caruso. It looks as though you might be at a celebration.

January 18, 2019

Hi Mom,

How are you today? I miss you more than words may express. How is Heaven? Is it easier for you to move around? Does God have all of your favorite foods up there? Each morning, as I soak in the beauty of the sunrise, I always think of you. I am not sure if it is because on Saturday, a couple of days before you left us and shattered our hearts into pieces, Annette and I sat there talking and visiting while you were sleeping. The sun was shining so brightly into your hospital window that we actually took pictures with our phones. We both agreed that the silver lining was completely stunning. Now, in retrospect, I wonder if you were already making arrangements with God, or Grandma and Grandpa, visiting with them in your dreams. At one point, the sun came through the clouds and what appeared was a golden path, which extended back up to heaven. Was God showing you the way home? I am sure He was. It was so beautiful. Sometimes, Mom, I wish I could take an escalator to heaven so I may give you kisses on your cheeks, hold you and let you know how much I love you. Even as I write this sentence, I cry, cry and cry asking God to help me.

My heart's desire was to fix everything, I wanted to come up with a viable solution. I wanted you to live into your nineties, with great ease and enjoy every Moment of living. Am I selfish? Guilty as charged. Yes, Mom, you were the nucleus that held everything and everyone together. You, Miss America, were the life of the party. I miss hearing your voice and having you dominate the conversation, without allowing me to get a word in edgewise. Mom, I'd give anything to hear your voice and to have you tell me about how many numbers you waited on at Bingo.

Yes, I walk around this world with a brave front, however, I miss you terribly. Mom, how does one say goodbye? I do not believe I shall ever say goodbye. For some reason, there are no instruction manuals on how to say goodbye to your Mom. While you were here on this planet, you never really said goodbye to your Mom either.

Each Memorial Day you would go to the graves and place flowers on grandma's tomb, along with your Dad's and other relatives. You must be having a grand time visiting with everyone. If by chance, you are able to read this in the spiritual realm, please give everyone a hug and kiss from me. January 22, 2019, is a few days away and I already cannot believe you are not here for me to wish you a Happy 78th birthday.

I've learned how to truly treasure life now, Mom. Not to say, I did not treasure it when you were here with me. However, I did not think you would leave us so quickly. I would have spent every Moment in October with you had I realized this. God let me know on October 17, 2018, that you were heading home on that Monday morning. I said, God, not now, please let her live longer.

Mommy, I guess you really wanted to go home as well. You spent most of the time in the hospital for the last three months of your life. I apologize for the behavior of some of the doctors, nurses, social workers and CNA's who were not the most kind or professional people when they worked with you.

Families need to know that their loved ones are taken very good care of. This was my primary reason for being there with you all day. I knew if these people realized you have family that love you and are visiting you often and on top of your care, they could not possibly mistreat you.

The meds did not help much either. If I had to do everything all over again, we would have let you stay at home and not given you those meds. I would have moved back to Boston for a while and taken care of you. Dad did not let us know how serious it was. He wanted to take care of you for as long as he could at home. How precious. He was correct, some of those CNA's in the nursing home were playing games on their phones instead of taking care of you. To know that the head of the nursing home allowed you to fall out of your bed four times onto a floor with a very thin mat was heartbreaking. What do these people get paid to do? Nothing? To torture the elderly, when, in fact they should be caring for you and countless others with utter respect and adoration.

Where has the moral fabric of this society gone? Mom, your health insurance pays for the salaries of these doctors, nurses, CNAs, and social workers. I know God is just and each person who was not kind to you shall be repaid in full. I am not holding any grudges, I wish them all well. However, there is a universal law, whatever one gives out, he/she shall receive it back 100 fold. Thus, it is of the upmost importance to give out kindness.

Mommy, I was and still am, completely honored to have spent those last few days with you. I was honored to hold the hand, who on countless occasion's held my little hand in hers. The beautiful Woman who walked with such dignity and strength, showing no fear in a neighborhood filled with conflicted and confused teenagers and young adults. All attempting to find their place in this world, embedded in a culture and climate of immense racism. You loved your mulatto children and your husband to no end and we all loved you even more. I loved the fact that color did not matter to you, but rather the content of the individuals character. Once someone became your friend, the person was a friend for life. Even as we went off to school and brought friends home from time to time, each one of my friends remembers how warm, kind and loving you were. All of them say without hesitation how they remember having some of your incredibly delicious homemade Italian sauce and how you kept filling their plate until they were utterly stuffed. Thank you Mom for treating my friends so kindly.

Mom, I often remember your comments of sharing with strangers once I wished them an absolutely wonderful life on every level, how you said, she is my poet. I thought and still think it is cute, even though I have never written a word of poetry. Here I go…..

Poem for Mom

Hair, dark brown and smooth, eyes brown as the earth, with a sparkle brighter than any star. A smile as priceless as any act of wonder. Hands, radiating out love to endless generations. Hugs are the best on this side of heaven. Words laced with love, stern instruction at times, and stories galore. Little Roman, (this is what Dad called you), he shares how his commanding officer is gone and no one is here to order him around.

I often picture you skirting around the floors in heaven, with no inhibitions, no issues at all with your legs, knees. You are whisking around everywhere.

Mom, if I had a billion life times to live, I would choose you as my Mom, every-time. You are simply the Most Incredible Mom Ever, in all of the world and beyond.

Grieving

Mom, I am heading home to visit with Dad today. I am confident you are aware at how hard it is for him to be here without you. Johnny is having a really hard time as well. I think it is because he did not have a chance to say goodbye. A few weeks ago, I finally made the decision to honor you with my life instead of being so upset that you are no longer here in the physical form. I begged God just for one Moment to create an escalator to heaven so I may see you, give you endless kisses on your face and know that you are happy, no longer in pain and visiting with your Mom who you loved more than life itself. I am so grateful for Grandma, she taught you how to love fiercely and this love now resides in all of our hearts.

I am confident you would like us to live our lives fully as you showed us how when you were on the planet. I am choosing to remember and to be grateful for being extremely blessed for having an extraordinary Mom like you. Mom, some people go their entire lifetimes and never have the privilege of experiencing a Mother's undying love for her children. I am grateful for the unconditional love, selfless giving of your time, energy and resources. I am amazed at how you did not allow not having learned to drive to hinder you. You would go out into the cold, the Northeasters in Boston, early in the morning, work long hours only to return to us (as Johnny remembers), with Chinese food. I must admit every place in Boston reminds me of you.

Thank you Mom for sending me to Modeling school as a teenager because you wanted me to realize how incredibly beautiful I am. I promise you Mom, your payment of those classes shall not be in vain. I tell myself each day that I am gorgeous and everyone loves me. I am honored to be a mixture of three incredible nationalities and I love my skin, hair, facial features, eyes, height, I love everything about me Mom. Why? You may ask? Because you have taught me that I am perfect exactly as I am. Thank you for this Mom. This knowledge has been the fuel to propel me on toward my goals and inner heart's dreams. I have never read this or heard of it before, however, after your passing, these words of wisdom have settled into my soul, as your undying love has.

A Mother's love is like a blanket that encircles a newborn's soul and remains as an insulator throughout that child's adult life forever. A Mother's love is the souls moral compass, leading the offspring aright. A Mother who believes and trusts in God as much as you do, is an added on eternal blessings.

Thank you Mom for introducing me to God while still in your womb. The God of Abraham, Issac and Jacob who has been and continues to be the Savior of our souls, my guiding light, my compass, my strength, shield, provider, deliverer, the lifter of my cup. I am so eternally grateful for all of the endless prayers you have prayed over my life and I may only believe you are still praying in heaven.

I am truly grateful for having the honor and privilege of spending the summer and fall months with you ;and then to pray over your body prior to anyone arriving to say goodbye to your outer shell. All of the doctors and nurses were amazed at how I cherished you.

A Word from the Love of Your Life

Well Mom, Dad is being shy. He misses you beyond what words may express. His entire world is empty and really I believe no longer has much meaning.

Understandably, it has been very difficult for him to go through your things and I have resumed those responsibilities. Please know, that it is not easy for me either, however, it has given me an even more sacred window in viewing the contents of your heart. Mom, you literally kept everything, how precious. Every card any of us ever sent you including cards from your sister Katy, Aunt Flo, Aunt Julie, Marcia, Lacye, your granddaughter, Leeanne. I found the pictures you hid in the closet so that I could not take them from you. I also found a precious picture of you at the age of six standing beside Auntie Katy. How beautiful. Even as a child Mom, you are so stunning, you are/ were definitely beyond modeling material.

Mom, here is Dad's rendition of how you both met each other.

"Met at the laundry mat. Aunt Katy was wild and I knew it. I decided to date Barbie instead. She was more peaceful, stayed at home, did not run the streets and took good care of your Grandmother, Anna Maria. Your Mom told me that black folks go with black folks and white folks go with white folks. Then, I told her I am going to marry you anyway because you're prejudice. Then, she told me, no you are not. I said, yes I am, you are going to be my wife.

When I met your Mom she had real long hair and would roll it up and place it in a ball on top of her head. She was cute and she knew she was cute.'

Wait a minute Dad, you may have needed spectacles back then, Mom was flat out stunning gorgeous and Praise God she knew it, because years later, she would have a mulatto little girl. She told me how gorgeous I am, when small minded people who were jealous and racist attempted to say differently.

Dad: 'I was poorer than two snakes, it did not stop your Mom from dating me. I was 18 and she was 19, we stayed together and I am not sure how we stayed together. Your Mom was pregnant with your brother Jimmy at 19 and gave birth to Jimmy when she turned 20. In the laundry mat where we met, she used to work with the binder machine that would fold the clothes and place a bow on it. She would always say that if I lived in a match box, she would live there with me, as long as we were together."

Endless Tears

Mom, I have not written in your book for a few weeks. I guess I cannot begin to allow the facts to settle into my soul. I still want to pick up the phone and call you. I still miss hearing your voice. Mom, why does no one ever share of how hard it is to lose your Mom? I know we all pass away one day, however, you were the love that binds all of our hearts together. Mom, you were the reason for everything. You loved each of us with the most incredible undying love I have ever witnessed in this life time thus far.

It has been snowing for the last twenty - four (24) hours and the snow drifts pile up quickly. I am tempted to head back outside to shovel more, plow more. I am heading out of town for two weeks for work. I am very thankful to be gainfully self-employed. I thank God for opening the doors for my inspirational speaking career and the way so many souls hearts are healed as a result of reading these words. Next month shall be the first time ever in my life that I do not hear your beautiful voice singing Happy Birthday to me.

I love you Mom. I wish I could have given you a much better life. I wish I could hit the rewind button and be a better friend to you as your daughter. Life is a funny thing, sometimes we rush through so fast that we do not realize that the most important people are right there waiting patiently for us to call and talk to them. You made the life you desired. You stayed married to the love of your life and were very proud of all of us. You were simply amazing Mom and shall always be simply amazing to me forever.

I love sunrises and sunsets. I remember the day before you passed away, there was the most spectacular silver lining that turned into a stream of light, as though there was a light illuminating the road all the way to heaven. A carpet of light rolled out especially for you.

Morning of your passing

The morning of your passing, I sent a message to one of my best friends, who lives in Salzburg, Austria. I copied the message and sent it to all family and friends everywhere. My heart was overwhelmed with sorrow and immense gratitude for having been so blessed to have a Mom like you.

My precious friend Helga.... yesterday morning at 6:47 a.m I lost the love of my life.

The person who held me as I came into the world, my biggest cheerleader, my confidant . How may I ever thank her for all that she has done for me? How do I tell her that she means the world to me and beyond. As I visited with her over the Summer months, watching this incredibly, strong, gorgeous and Fearless woman go through one of the most challenging times of her precious life... all I kept praying is God, please heal her. My precious friend Helga, I kissed my Mom's face and cheeks endlessly, giving her great big hugs and telling her how she is the Most Incredible Mom ever. Truly, Helga, there is nothing like a Mother's love. Nothing more fierce. My Mother loved us and my Dad with a fierce love, an undying love, she would never give up on us. It was my honor to literally hold her hand each day during this time. This precious hand, who fed, clothed and cuddled me as a baby, child and even as an adult. While visiting her once at the hospital, I was talking and some water went down the wrong pipe. She, even in her state, sat up in the bed, pulled herself up so quickly and pulled me toward her patting me on the back to clear my throat . I was amazed and began to tear up. Even in her sickness, she still emerges as that Fearless Mom, I have come to admire and am so honored to have the privilege to be born of such an incredible (and believe me the English vernacular does not have a word to describe her undying love), exceptional human being. I am honored, proud and humbled to call her Mom. I love you FOREVER. For all eternity Mommy.

Thank you my precious friend for allowing me to share about my precious, truly precious Mother. God bless you ... Your friend, Ann Marie

Mom, I had the most incredible dream last night. I dreamt that you came back, you were walking and had on a very nice blue dress, a similar color to one I own. You wanted to have Dad sleep in the same bed and asked me to go fetch him from the community apartments he had moved into. For some reason you wanted to know if the postal services were still open in the grocery store we happen to be in . I said, no Mom, it is past 9:30 pm, they are all closed now. Then, as I headed up these stairs to fetch Dad, I looked behind me and there you were in the grocery store buying stamps and driving a blue car. Amazing, walking and driving and you looked simply gorgeous. I was a little protective because I noticed you were running a slight fever and I wanted you to rest. I found Dad and shared your wishes, he went upstairs to his room to gather his belongings and before he could reach the top of the stairs, I peered out the window and soaked in a beautiful scene of the clefts with the ocean dashing against the rocks. I stopped on the stairs and said, Dad, Mom loves you more than life itself. She has come back to be with her true love. I shared at how I must write a book about her love for you. You are and shall ever be the Love of Her Life. I miss you Mom, thank you for coming into my dreams last night to visit me and express your endless love for Dad.

I found this picture while viewing all of the picture in your album that you hid in the closet to prevent us from helping ourselves to the pictures while you were still alive. There is your incredible smile, the smile that lights up the world and any room you enter. I love you Mom, I love how you instilled in us how to appreciate each day of our lives and to love and honor God. I am particularly fond of the picture hanging behind you, I believe I fell in love with the Impressionist period due to passing by this picture in the hallway at our home on countless occasions.

Mom, I wish you were here so that I may give you a hug and lots of kisses on your cheeks. I loved to witness your facial expression as we lavished you with tons of kisses. The love you showed us as your children is a blanket of love that carries us through even one of the toughest times of our lives of loosing you. Thank you for being the utter definition of love. There is a saying that goes something like this…when a person has children they grow in their capacity to love deeply. Quite honestly Mom, I believe the opposite, I believe you were borne with immense amounts of endless love and when God allowed you to bear children, the love permeated within your soul to the point of overflowing into ours. Our cup runneth over Mom, our cup runneth over. You truly are one of the Best Mom's anyone could ever wish to have in any lifetime.

Mom, naturally, I admire how you and Dad stayed together inspite of all of the civil unrest of the 1960's. I may truly say that none of us children ever even knew what color was because we grew up in a household filled with love.

Even, when you attempted to explain to us how some people dislike others due to the color of their skin, none of us could even begin to comprehend this sad notion. I remember the a certain militant group standing outside of our home and looking up at us while we played on the porch. I thought to myself, why don't they like my Mom, she clearly likes all races and this is evident with who she married.

Mom, you were so brave…both you and Dad to be in love at such a time as then and to allow your love for each other to last a lifetime. Mom, how blessed were you to have the chance to spend your entire life, with the love of your life. Most people would love to experience even half or a fraction of such good fortune.

Mom, Dad misses you so much. I really wish there were some way his heart could be consoled. He shares stories of when you both met, how, since he was raised by his uncle since his Mom and Dad passed when he was a little boy, you were everything to him. I often remind him of how incredibly blessed he is to have the privilege and honor to have been married to you. Your love mended our hearts, provided fuel for our dreams and allows each one of us to Soar as on Wings of Eagles. Mom, I know our love for you provided the same. I shall always remember the day before your passing and how you wanted me to call Dad on FaceTime. I stared intently at you as you sat there quietly taking in every crevice of Dad's face, his voice, each millimeter of the FaceTime image of Dad. It was almost as if you were recording his voice, his image so that you would remember and not forget when in heaven.

I sat there completely intrigued and amazed. I knew for certain that that Sunday would be your last day with us, as God had told me months prior and then on that Friday night close to midnight when I flew in to visit you in the ICU. As soon as you were able to speak on Sunday morning after the nurse removed the breathing apparatus, you said, in your commanding voice, Call Jimmy Now. I smiled and said to myself, 'The Queen is on the Throne'.

Mom, I feel incredibly honored to have had those precious Moment with you. I am thankful for each word, each compliment you gave….even then at the last Moments of your life, there you are letting us know how much you love us. You took my Iphone out of my hands and brought the phone to your lips to kiss Dad. I started to cry. Earlier, when we first called Dad you said, I want a french fry. I knew for certain, that you were asking for your favorite food and would be leaving us too soon.

Mom, I need some alone time…a trip to Italy, in particular to Sicily as I promised you when you were alive. I wish to see the place where your Mother was born and walk on the same streets she may have walked on as a little girl. Then I wish to travel to Naples where your Dad was born and do the same.

I wish you were here with me to travel to your native land. I call Italy the country that exudes love. Every precious Italian soul I have ever met when traveling through Italy has always been lovely to meet and visit with.

Sometimes, Mom, I do not understand life. I do not understand why someone as wonderful as you, had to go so soon. I think I am going to write the rest of this at home, as I have a tendency to cry when I am writing this beautiful dedication to you.

I woke up one Saturday morning really early. For some reason I could not sleep, as my mind was steadfast on you. As I peered out my window, I saw this remarkable scenery, the night was receding as the dawn approached. Simply spectacular, Mom. I often wonder what you are able to witness now that you are in the spirit form. Have you seen God, have you hugged Jesus? Are all of our loved ones there? Are you talking with them and visiting? If you are, please give everyone a hug and kiss from me. I pray all the time, however, if you are able to approach God, please give Him a nice long hug from me and a kiss. Let Him know that I am so appreciative and eternally grateful to Him for giving me such an Extraordinary Mom as you. I love you Mom, forever.

Mom, I walked into my local library the other day and noticed this plaque. I was simply amazed. Last summer, prior to you becoming seriously ill, you said to a couple of people when we were awaiting your cataract surgery that, 'She is my Poet.' after I wished a few nice people a Wonderful Life on Every Level. Instinctively, again Mom, you knew something on a deeper level that I realized. All of my life, ever since I was 10, I loved walking over to our local library in Brighton (it is still there to this day) and read the Writers magazines. My heart was drawn to writing and I wished to write many books to inspire people's souls all over the world even then as I am actually doing today. Thank you Mom, for your confirmation, so many years later.

The picture above was taken on Sunday, the day when most of the world celebrates the Risen Christ. Easter Sunday, Mom. This was your favorite holiday, as it is the day our Lord rose from the dead. The sky is ablaze as the sun starts to set on this day. Mom, I always run to the window even more now to capture the sunrises and sunsets. When Annette and I were sitting in your hospital room two days before you went to heaven, there was one of the most gorgeous silver linings in the sky. I explained to Annette what it meant. Then, a little later, I noticed a golden road, which looked like it was leading up to heaven. I believe God was opening the gates of heaven in anticipation of your beautiful arrival.

Mom, I love the way the clouds appear in this photo. I took several pictures from my upstairs deck. This one looks like God was painting the clouds into the backdrop of the sky. God is definitely the Master painter, creating all creation and each of us as His masterpiece. I am so grateful for you Mom, you were one of His truly special and treasured masterpieces.

Journey to Italy to pay Tribute to Your Life Mom.

Where shall I begin. Mom, I really wish I had taken the trip to Palermo, Sicily and Naples Italy prior to your passing. I wish I could have sent you the post card you so desired, to finally answer your very profound question of whether or not the mailing address on the postcard would be post marked, Palermo Sicily or Sicily Italy. I have arrived back home now and two weeks have passed, and the post card I mailed from there has not arrived yet.

I am amazed at what happens to a soul when one loses someone as near and dear to their heart as their Mom. I am convinced that God created Mom's with an extra measure of love, tenacity and fierceness to love and protect their offspring whether in the human or animal kingdom.

When you passed in October, 2018, I felt such a loss and still do to this day. I often wish to pick up the phone and talk to you, I miss your voice. I miss sneaking up on you and Dad in Boston and hearing the surprise in your voice and your laughter as I cover your precious face in tons of kisses. Mom, your laughter was infectious. You, lit up the home and our lives with your love and laughter.

As I promised you in my heart, I sailed for Italy at the end of May to deposit your hair in both places where your parents were borne. The morning of my departure, as I brushed my hair, I could not believe I was heading on this pilgrimage to say goodbye to your physical life lived while on this earth. (I firmly believe that you are with me always, as I feel your presence and see your love everywhere I go), as you shall see in the latter body of this story.

As I brushed my hair, this thought came over me and said, I must not let your hair go to Sicily and Naples alone. I want to be there with you so that you will not get lost or feel alone, so I gathered some of my hair from my brush and joined it with yours.

Mom, writing this book is the second hardest thing I have to do, each time I write about you, tears start to stream down my cheeks to the point that I am no longer able to read the words on the pages.

Boarding the plane

Amazingly enough, the flight went by relatively quickly for a 7 hour flight and I found myself navigating my way through the Shipol airport in Amsterdam to catch my connecting flight to Barcelona. The lines are incredibly long there to pass through the immigration line and often passengers are stressed to the max, attempting to make their connecting flight. Nevertheless, the process is so fast paced, that no one has a chance to dose off. Which I believe, in retrospect is a wise, 'built-in' feature. (I love you my Cookie Crumb!!!)

As I awaited my connecting flight, again, I met really nice people from all over Europe and America and wished them a lovely life. One lady was traveling to Barcelona for work. The gentleman that sat next to me on the flight was quite lovely. He worked for Mercedes Benz, I believe he may have been one of their Senior Vice Presidents, a really nice fellow. He was facilitating a training session for their top customers to learn how to operate one of the newest models designed by his company.

We had a lovely conversation about the snow covered mountains and all of the nice places to visit in Barcelona. I made my way through the airport after being in the passport line.

Finally made it to the ship, the reception crew directed us to the Cheri Lounge where the welcome reception was. I wish I had known we were attending such a lavish reception with plenteous appetizers and champagne, along with sparkling water and sodas. I would have skipped breakfast. There was a lovely band playing and again, I began to tear up inside as I sat there taking in all of the beauty of the Moment, wishing you were there to experience this with me. On some level, I know you were there. Beaming with your most beautiful smile, I have had the pleasure of basking in my entire life.

I believe when I booked the trip, it was in January, shortly after your birthday and I knew I had to do this to pay tribute to your most beautiful life. I was petrified, since I never traveled via a cruise in my life. So, I ensured my room and balcony were large enough to allow me to breathe and have space away from the rest of the guests on the ship. Often, I would go out on the balcony to talk to you and watch the sunset or sunrise. I cherished my privacy and the freedom to cry as I thought of you and how I finally am embarking on the journey to both Sicily and Naples.

My first excursion was in Genova, Italy. Mom, I find each part of Italy, whether I am in Milano, Florence or Pisa, simply beautiful. I may say the same for Genova. This particular excursion was your own walking tour without a guide through the city of Genova. I took a picture of the art museum as my landmark and being the Bostonian that I am and possessing such a spirit of adventure, I proceeded through the charming streets of Genova

The excursion tour lady shared on our bus ride over to the bus stop, that there was a lovely pesto shop that made the pesto right there in front of you. As I ventured through the town, I noticed that a number of the shops had not opened yet, as it was only 10:00 am.

Upon the end of my walk, I viewed the map and headed in the direction of the Pesto place. I walked over to where I thought the place would be to discover it was not there. Finally, after walking a little further I asked some waitresses in this restaurant if they knew where this place was. One of the waitress understood English very well (see Mom, you should have taught us all Italian!!!). She pointed me in the right direction. To my utter surprise, I had walked by the place on an earlier personal guided tour of Genova. I do not believe it was open at that time.

Mom, look at this pesto (It is simply delicious) They made the pasta right there as well. Bellissimo.

I sat at the table that had a huge window, facing the beautiful apartment building next to the shop and part of the street. I wondered in my heart what it would feel like living in Italy, overlooking the ocean. Basking in the aroma of the garlic, fresh basil and pine nuts soaked in olive oil, I completely enjoyed every last bite of the pesto. I also purchased some focaccia bread with the fresh pesto to bring back with me to the ship. Delicio.

As I strolled back through the streets of Genova, I soaked in the beauty of the town, the fruit stand, the vendors with various trinkets (some native to Italy, others native to lands far away).

On the way back to the square, I found a rest room area which was enclosed in an enchanting mall. I browsed through the enchanting shops and felt led to wait until I arrived in Sicily and Naples to purchase T-shirts and other gifts.

On my way back to where the Bus would pick us up, I discovered a gelato stand and treated myself to a cone. In the sweltering heat, I walked over to an outside market and viewed the merchandise all the way up to the Art Museum. I decided to purchase a bar of lavender soap as the soap on the ship was in a metal container and one necessarily did not feel completely clean when washing in it. The nice thing Mom, was that the soap came along with a beautiful face cloth with Genova written on it.

Arriving back at the ship in time for dinner was perfect. I dropped off my items to the cabin and headed for the dining hall. Mom, I discovered that the cruise line dropped the itinerary in your mailbox the same evening at 9:00 pm. The itinerary lists the next port we would visit the following day. Now, for some reason, I did not read the front page and went to the middle of the bulletin to read which bus I had to board for my particular excursion. It was the Island of Capri. I believe you mentioned that your Dad's family was from there? It is simply gorgeous.

Naples, Italy

I awoke the next morning with my heart racing a bit, with my hair intertwined with yours, I read the front page of the bulletin, only to read, "Welcome to Naples." A little nervous, excited, yet very remorseful at the same time..I knew this was the first step in my tribute to you as my Mom, (the Most Excellent Mom in all of the world) and I did not want to start the process. Instead, everything within my soul screamed, God, I know you can raise her from the dead and heal her completely and give her back to me and our family. God, this must be a mistake, she departed from us too soon. Please, please, please God bring her back. You, God, can do anything. Mom, I wanted to turn back the clock of time. Turn back time from 20 years ago, when you were completely healthy, without a care in the world.

I do have the faith that God can raise you from the dead, however, I believe He is not ready to do so until the entire world bows down and makes Jesus Christ, Lord and Savior of their lives.

Prior to boarding the shuttle, I said a prayer and walked over to the ocean which was right outside the City of Naples and stood there, reciting a silent prayer to myself. I prayed Mom, for God to please take very good care of you in heaven and to remember to give you lots of hugs and kisses to remind you of how much I love you and to tell you that you are most certainly "'My Cookie Crumb." I asked God to please be with our hair as I placed your hair with mine intertwined with yours, into the ocean. I said a silent prayer of goodbye. Mom, I did not want your hair to feel lonely or to get lost traveling through Italy, this is why I intertwined mine with yours, to keep you company always.

Island of Capri

Our excursion tour guide was a really nice gentleman who assured us we would be able to sit upstairs in the quieter section of the ferry once it departed.

True to his promise, I walked up the stairs and found a somewhat empty ferry and chose a seat by the window soaking in the view. Other members from my excursion group joined me upstairs. As I disembarked from the ferry, there in front of me awaited the Island of Capri

Mom, Capri is simply gorgeous, there are Lemon trees everywhere and the sky this particular day was clear blue with the royal blue color of the ocean underneath and the beautiful bright sunshine shining overhead. The views were simply spectacular, I purchased a lift ticket to take me up to the top of the mountain of the Island of Capri. I felt your love with me, Mom, every step of the way.

On the way up the side of the mountain, I noticed another excursion guide from our ship who was taking his group on a walking tour. I asked him if I may join them and he happily invited me along. We walked along the streets at a very quick pace and stayed with him up until the garden, visited the beautiful garden and then I decided to explore the Island on my own.

Mom, in our ancestral line and in honor of you, I purchased a beautiful dress from Capri that represents the beautiful blue sky, the water, the gorgeous lemon trees and the sunshine; in addition to purchasing a beautiful white blouse and a simply gorgeous blue shirt which I wore in my travels to Ibiza. I shall include a picture later.

I enjoyed yet another gelato and walked around a little more after my purchases. Mom, being surrounded by all of these native Italians, the aroma of exquisite Italian food flooding the airwaves, I felt at home, basking in the beauty of my culture. A culture you allowed me to experience when you met Dad and decided to spend your life with him, regardless of his color. Mom, you never saw color, you loved Dad and all of us for who we are. Thank you Mom, for loving us so. I love soaking in the beauty of this Island, on some level, I feel as though you are sending me your love.

Heading back down the trolley that carried us up to the top of the Island, I visited the shops on the lower level of the island and purchased a really neat t-shirt of the Island of Capri, some lemon candies and then as I met our excursion gentleman, I, along with a couple of others were the first to arrive at the meeting spot, we had some time, so I walked up the road a little ways to spot a woman sitting outside of this Italian restaurant having a delicious pizza with her young son. I asked if it was fabulous and she said yes. I quickly went inside and talked to the owner who assured me that they may make an authentic Italian pizza within 7 minutes. I said perfect, ordered it and walked back to the group. I returned later to pick up my pizza and enjoyed a slice prior to boarding the shuttle. Mom, this is the best Italian pizza I have ever tasted in my entire life, here on the precious Island of Capri. Mom, look at how lovely this pizza looks, believe me it tasted superb. I know you would have enjoyed every bite.

Your Original Question

Mom, if you remember a few years prior to your becoming ill, you asked me what I considered and still consider a profound question. 'Would my post card read, Palermo Sicily or Sicily Italy?' I purchased several post cards and mailed one to myself and one to Johnny. I have not received it in the mail yet…however, as soon as it arrives I shall have your answer.

As all of the passengers boarded the ferry, I looked back and said a silent "Thank you" to the Island of Capri.

Mom, again, I believe God predestined this trip. The other day, I was visiting with a treasured friend of mine explaining how I recently traveled to Italy to deposit your hair with mine intertwined in Naples and Palermo Sicily. I explained how our hair is at this sanctuary and when my friend "Google earthed" it, the landmark of the sanctuary is in the shape of a heart.

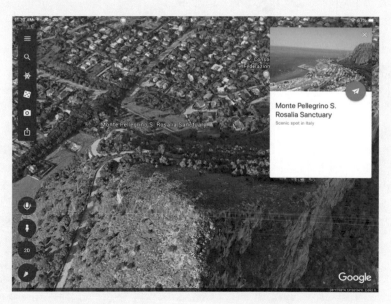

Mom, I was simply blown away when I received her picture from the aerial view and I began to sob. Every single detail God ordained. He knows how much you speak to my soul through hearts and unbeknownst to me, I had no idea why I was drawn to this particular excursion. I thought it would be nice to see the sanctuary and then as the bus headed up this steep mountain side, providing the most beautiful aerial view of Palermo, I felt this thought within my heart to deposit our hair here. I placed our hair in the fence behind the heart shaped stone a friend of mine gave me as a Memorial of My love to you.

As I proceeded up the long stair case, I treasured each step, as I had the honor of walking up the stairs of so many of my ancestors, who ascended this mountain to offer up prayers for our loved ones and so many more precious souls all over the world. My heart overflowed with tears of having such an honor to participate in this enormous event. While climbing the stairs, I noticed a beggar and thought, my, how did this person get up the mountain, it was a very long way to walk even for the fittest of individuals. I gave him a few Euros, Mom, his heart was truly grateful.

Mom, I am convinced, life is filled with countless treasures and precious people to be a witness and friend to those treasures. You, my love were one of those treasures and shall always live forever in my heart. I love you Mom - Forever!!!!

As I listened to the tour guide explain the historical facts about the sanctuary, I was truly amazed to discover it is called a Sanctuary of Prayer. God is completely priceless and Sovereign, of all of the places in Sicily to be drawn to, was this beautiful Sanctuary of Prayer! I know you would have loved this place as well and the saint who fed the poor people of Palermo.

I walked in, soaking in the beauty and holiness of the sanctuary, embracing the serenity of all of the precious souls who traveled here from around the world to provide endless gifts for this particular Saint's ministry.

When I initially arrived on the ship, I had no idea where I would place your hair with mine . I prayed and asked God to grant me guidance and success on this trip. As I viewed the different excursions, I noticed there was a sanctuary at the top of the highest mountain in Palermo, Sicily. My heart was instantly drawn there and I knew I had to ascend the mountain and place our hair in this sanctuary.

I had planned to deposit our hair along the mountain side on the way up to the Sanctuary, overlooking Palermo, Sicily. However, this ever present 'gentle thought' said wait and look at the interior and exterior of the Sanctuary and the grounds first.

I marveled at the interior and walked to the very front and knelt down and said a prayer for you in front of the statue of Jesus (our Lord and Savior). I then, stood up and walked over to a pew and sat there for a while, crying quietly as I soaked in the reality that I made it here, finally, to Palermo, Sicily, the birthplace of my Grandma, your precious Mom, whom you loved more than life itself. Wow, generations upon generations of my Italian ancestors probably made the journey up to this sanctuary. My friend Beverly (who shared the picture of the aerial view) pointed out that the sanctuary is known as a Sanctuary of Prayer.

Again, as she shared this information I began to cry. All I could think about was all of the years you prayed to God for everything in our lives and how incredible the power of prayer is. Thank you Mom, for showing me how to pray and being an example of the power of answered prayers in our lifetime together. I shall continue to pray and give all honor and glory to God for the very existence of you.

Your love Mom, has given me and my siblings the power to Soar through life. We are all level headed, strong and (some of us more opinionated than others…smile) Thank you Mom for loving us so fiercely. I know now that this is the way God has created Mothers. Mothers are the 'glue' that binds the family together with love as the sealant over our hearts. Thank you God for giving us all a glimpse of how You love each and everyone of us.

Mom, look at how beautiful this sanctuary is. I knew you would love it.

I knelt here in front of the altar on the right hand side and said a silent prayer of blessing on your entire life; I thanked God for giving me a Mom like you. I shared again, how, if I had to choose a billion times over, who my Mom would be, I would choose you every single time Mom!!!!!! Tears rolled down my cheeks and I stood up and walked to the bench in front of the sanctuary, surprised that there were not tons of people around, I sat there and just worshipped the Lord in this beautifully peaceful place, wondering in my mind if our ancestors sat in this very sanctuary and prayed prayers for our family, of generations past. I asked God to bless every single soul who has ever entered here and whoever shall. May each soul give their lives over to the Lord Jesus forever.

The Day at Sea was my third day after I had placed our hair in both Naples and Palermo Sicily. I mentioned to my friend Leah, if I should cut my hair, as it blew endlessly in the wind. Leah said, if you find a pair of scissors, I shall gladly cut it for you.

I finished our walk and headed downstairs to have some spritzer water with Leah, only to have an older Italian gentleman visit our table and point his two fingers to his face and say in (broken English), you look Italiano. I said yes, and then, Mom he proceeded to talk to me endlessly in Italian. I listened intently and then he said he was hungry and would get some food and come back to the table to join us.

I looked around on the deck and there were multiple empty tables where he could have sat. There were others sitting and visiting at tables as well. I mentioned this to my friend Leah, who he kept referring to as being French. We both chuckled, since she is from England. I explained to my friend Leah, how, although I am not hungry, I shall get a small plate of food and join the older Italian gentleman, because I know from growing up in my culture, Italians do not wish to eat alone. He returned to the table with a few plates of food (salad, main dish and a dessert). I thought, I shall eat only a small amount and then politely excuse ourselves, as I needed to go in pursuit of those scissors. Mom, he ended up showing us pictures of his family, and then showed me in his cell phone his niece Anna Maria's name and phone number. How priceless. He thanked us for visiting with him and I headed on my way.

I visited a few places on the ship to see if they had scissors. Finally, the photo shop had a pair they could spare, I called my friend Leah from one of the ship's phone and headed to her cabin. For the next two hours, this precious soul, referred back to your picture to style my hair the same way.

All of my hair that was cut off was placed in a small white bag, the hair from the towel and some that fell on the floor was gathered up. My friend Leah, had a small handful of my hair that she went to scatter in the ocean from her balcony. She came back inside and said, Ann Marie, I attempted to scatter your hair in the ocean, however, it went straight up into the sky. I thought that was peculiar. As I headed back to my cabin and went out to my balcony to do the same thing, the entire bag of hair I now had in my hands went straight up into the sky as well. I thought to myself and later shared with my friends that you, Mom, must have asked God for a vacuum cleaner to vacuum all of my hair up to heaven to be with you.

Traveling to Ibiza, Spain

On our walking tour through Ibiza, which is simply a beautiful place as well, Mom. I noticed a little old Italian lady in our walking group with her husband, who may have needed my help navigating those cobblestone streets and steep hills. So, I took it upon myself to help her. She was so sweet, Mom, she spoke to me in Italian, thank goodness for the Italian Speaking CD's I listen to. I was able to understand most of what she was communicating as well as most of the things her husband shared as well. Lot's of finger and hand gestures work beautifully too.

Once we listened to the Tour guide explain how to take the shuttle bus back to the ship, I headed off for an adventure of Ibiza. I walked through the streets, went to various shops and had a very fine lunch at this new restaurant that recently opened. In a way, Mom, I felt honored to be one of her patrons, as I am a business owner myself, I felt that God allowed me to dine here, as with the Fish place in Palermo, Sicily to bless these new business owners. Below is a picture of the place in Palermo, Sicily, where the owner recently opened his new business. The fish was delicious.

The owner of the new restaurant in Ibiza, had a little boy, who was probably 4 or 5 years old. He had his little towel and cleaned the bathroom sinks, door knobs and tables very carefully. What a good business person, even at a young age. Later, he rode his little bike up and down the walk way. I, personally was happy to see how he possessed a great work/life balance.

Mom, I know you are not fond of calamari, however, this was one of the best dishes I have ever tasted. It was drizzled with fresh lemon and the finest Extra Virgin Olive Oil. I ordered a single pizza with a glass of red wine, in your honor, as I know how you loved a glass of red wine every once in a while.

Upon finishing my lunch, I decided to explore more of the Island of Ibiza. Our ship was scheduled to depart at 3:00 am in the morning, so this gave all of the passengers an opportunity to truly enjoy Ibiza without having to 'run' back to the ship at a certain time. After boarding the shuttle bus to head back to the ship, I noticed a beach within walking distance from the ship, and after dropping off my things, headed over to sit along the seashore.

I walked along the sidewalks, I discovered the distance from the ship to the beach was more than 10 minutes, and instead took 20 minutes. On my way, I met this nice young Italian couple from the ship who had the same idea in mind, spending time at the ocean.

We talked and discovered wonderful restaurants along the way to dine at later, if we felt so inclined. As we reached the beach, I said my farewell and continued to walk for miles along the seashore. It was as though my soul was taking in the reality that I had accomplished my promise to bringing a part of you to your Mom's and Dad's land.

I felt a sense of completion, as though this particular chapter in my book of life was completed. I walked a little farther along the seashore to find a place that had more sand than seaweed and plopped down on my towel. I captured the beauty of the sea, with all of its various shades of deep majestic blues and hues of green. Ah, what an Incredible God we serve, who makes such beauty, Mom!!!!!

The water was crystal clear and the ebb and flow of the tide drew me in. Noticing a jelly fish on my left, I navigated through the water to a place that had only sand, as I placed water on my face and arms, I noticed to my right some seaweed. Mom, it was in the shape of a heart. I knew instinctively this was you, giving me your sign of approval for the trip in honoring you. I cried and accepted the beauty of your love through the seaweed that was in the shape of a heart and snapped three pictures of the beautiful heart to etch this memory in my heart for eternity.

I shared with one of my precious friends how I believe God grants you permission to visit with us. Perhaps, you see how sad we feel and how much we miss you. Mom, I can picture you asking the King of the Universe, if you may have permission to have 'heaven leave', you know, similar to 'shore leave' and show up in hearts, not only in the ocean in seaweed, but in the sunset that next evening as well. Thank you for loving me so much to show me how much you love me. I love you to the Moon and Beyond Mom, to the Moon and Beyond!!!!!!

I believe, truly believe God allows you (Mom) to speak to me in the forms of my seeing hearts everywhere. Mom, this is the same friend that Googled the sanctuary in Palermo Sicily from Google Earth and saw that the sanctuary location from the aerial view was in the shape of a heart. She exclaimed that God has a sense of humor. Thus, I agree and truly do believe He grants you special permissions to encourage your loved ones on earth. Thank you for thinking of us Mom. You shall always live powerfully with immense love in my heart and soul.

On an intricately spiritual level Mom, I believe God orchestrated the entire journey. He led me to Palermo, Sicily (even though I was quite nervous to arrive there on a ship, since I normally travel by plane and visit on land and not via the sea). God knew our 'love message' to each other would be in the shape of a heart, even before our very souls showed up on the planet.

I believe God also had you ask me the daunting question of what a post card would read, 'Palermo, Sicily or Sicily Italy. As, your question planted the 'seed' in my heart to travel there and mail myself back a postcard to answer your question.

Mom, this statue was at the port in Palermo Sicily, as I studied her features, she resembled you in your twenties. The Timeless outstanding beauty that these gorgeous Sicilian women possess; I love what the statute represents, as if this is you, sending out beams of life, love and kindness to the entire world.

I imagined Grandma living on this street with her clothes hanging on the clothes line to dry.

Palma De Malleroca

Mom, you would have been so proud of me on this walking tour. This is the walking tour where Orbitz offered me a coupon and I only spent $8 to hop on and off the bus. Great bargain, right, Mom!

This city was simply breathtakingly beautiful and happened to be the place where God literally helped me find and purchase an outfit for the last evening of the cruise. I walked the beautiful streets of Palma and visited several shops, until I found one shop that had so many gorgeous dresses to choose from, I spent almost an hour trying on clothing.

I picked a beautiful full length long white dress, which was more beautiful and economical than a dress I almost purchased a few boutiques down the road.

Walking a little further, I discovered a lovely bakery, where I stopped to purchase a quick snack and took in the beauty of the area. On my way back into the main entrance, I discovered yet another store, which sold beautiful scarfs. I purchased a green one, the color of my eyes. Mom, you would have loved it. The color matched a bracelet I purchased earlier along with some pearl earrings that I wore for the evenings farewell party.

I am wearing the dress and scarf above, the picture next to yours with your fashionable short hairdo. (since the trip, I have learned Hebrew and will be wearing the white dress on the second year of your passing away to honor you, as I read the Torah portion of Noah. I am including my friend Tatyana's Mom in the honoring as her Mom passed

51

away two weeks after you did, (Mom. I am certain you both are best friends in heaven and orchestrated Tatyana and I meeting). I am also going to include my friend Greg Vacinek's Mom in the prayer as she passed a week prior to you, six years ago. All of us can truly understand the pain each other shares at the loss of our precious Moms.

Everyone complimented me and my friends from London, especially Bernie could not believe I purchased my entire outfit on my visit to Palma earlier in the day. The night was delightful, as our friend Bernie had entered 'The Voice of the Sea'. I knew instinctively she would win, as she chose the song from Etta James, 'At Last'. I thought to myself, no one in their correct mind would choose such a song, unless, of course they were truly skilled in singing.

To my utter enjoyment, she won. We all joined her for pizza on the 11th floor of the cruise ship to celebrate. Never thought I would be eating pizza at almost one in the morning.

From my Cabin on the Cruise ship - Fulfilling my Promise to Mom

Good evening Mom,

I miss you more than words may know. Today, I arrived in Naples, Italy and scattered your hair with mine intertwined in yours into the port in the City of Naples, as I boarded a ferry to the Island of Capri, where I believe you mentioned that Grandpa was born? As I held your hair in my hands, I placed the strands to my nostrils to smell your hair and beautiful aroma one last time.

Capri is simply breathtakingly beautiful, I saw a young lady on the ferry who looked exactly like you at the tender ago of twenty (20) and I sat there marveling at her exquisite beauty. I must admit, Mom, your gene pool is exceedingly strong as your Dad's is, there were a number of lovely Italian ladies that looked like you at various stages of your life.

Tomorrow, we head to Palermo, as I finished dinner in the dining area, I headed up to my cabin early to spend time on my balcony as the ship left port to say goodbye to Naples, I just needed to say a prayer to God to ask Him to take good care of you. Then, I thought, oh, I must go back and get our hair, I felt as though I was leaving you behind. Then, as I stood there crying, tears streaming down my face, a flock of seagulls appeared overhead following the wake of the boat. For some reason, this early evening, they seemed to sense my sadness and see the tears of sorrow streaming down my face. Instinctively, they knew they needed to fly really close to me, as if they were lifting me higher in their hearts, as if they offered up a special prayer to the Creator to say, please God, comfort her. It was beautiful Mom. I believe God has already embedded in life all of the kindness we need to carry us through the heartbreaks and loses of life. Each tear has a name, each tear is stored in a jar in heaven with my name on it.

I know God is showering down His favor on my life and our family and all of my precious friends. I know I shall be very successful in my self-employment. Well, my eyes are heavy and I have a full day in Palermo, Sicily tomorrow on which I shall purchase a post card and send it to my home to finally answer your precious questions from five or more years ago, and of which you asked me recently prior to you becoming ill, 'will the post card say, Palermo Sicily, or Sicily, Italy.

A very good question Mom, I shall let you know tomorrow. Sweet dream my Queen, you shall reign in my heart and soul for all eternity. I love you Mom! You are the Most Incredible Mom Ever!!!!!!

Best Gelato in Palermo, Sicily.

Mom, I know you already know your precious grandson Baby Fervin on the spiritual plane. Annette shares many of the dreams she has where you are visiting with her. I think it is simply beautiful how you still give her advice in her dreams and let her know recently not to worry, as God has everything under His control and it is all taken care of. I included a picture of your precious grandson at his first birthday celebration.

Mom, he is so strong, if I lived closer, I would not have to work out another day of my life, just chasing after him as he explores his world would keep me in tip top shape. (smile). He is such a genius, always figuring out how something works, imitating everything he sees his Mom and Dad do. Baby Fervin is a true genius.

Mom, as the ship left port, the sunset in Palermo, Sicily was in the shape of a heart. I knew, instinctively this was you, sending me a message of love.

Thank you Mom for sending me a heart shaped sunset.

Acknowledgements

I would like to thank Bonnie Johnson for offering to edit this precious book, as each time I attempted to, I began to cry, which prolonged the editing process. Thank you Bonnie for extending such an eternal kindness. I pray for God's blessings in your life and Clinton's forever.

Thank you to my Dad, who continued to remind me to send him a copy of the book, once complete. Thank you to Bonnie Olson Kramer and Bonnie Johnson and my Dad for insisting on my publishing the book to share with the world.

Thank you to my Mom (who's in Heaven) for placing all of this love in my heart and soul to radiate out into the world. Thank you and Dad for loving each other regardless of your ethnicity and showing me to do the same, to love and respect people of all nationalities. You truly are the most Incredible Mom Ever!!!!!

My Wish

....

It is my hearts desire and fervent wish that whoever reads this book will feel the immense love my Mother poured into my soul during her entire life. I pray that each one of you would experience, give and receive the undying love that only a Mother can give. May you experience this love in your most precious relationships, to believe in, speak words of encouragement and strength into your children's lives, into your parent's lives, into your spouses life, into your friends and neighbors lives; and yes, into your own life!

Printed in the United States
by Baker & Taylor Publisher Services